I0625947

The Truth is not Always What it Seems

By
Henry Joshua Garcia, MBA

ISBN
Hardcover:978-1-966565-54-3
Paperback:978-1-966565-55-0

A Message to My Son

Love comes from the depths of a father's heart, and at times, it may seem tough. But know that in those moments of tough love, I am truly expressing how much I care about the man you are becoming. This book serves as a foundation for you—a way to build a mindset and a way of thinking.

Go beyond what the world programs for you, for I am so proud of who you are. This book is an expression of my love and a testament to how you inspired me to share this message.

I love you always,

Dad!

Dedication

To my parents, who brought me into this world and did the best they could to raise a child who sought his own path. I know it wasn't always easy, but your efforts created a foundation that allowed me to discover my strength and pursue my dreams. Though I carved my own way, I am deeply grateful for the life you provided and the important lessons learned along the journey. Thank you for being a part of my story.

To my dearest wife, thank you for the boundless love and strength you share with me every day. Your unwavering commitment to caring for my heart and supporting my dreams means the world to me. Through every storm and celebration, you have stood by my side, lighting my path with your love. I look forward to the day when we can sit together, gazing at the stars in our old age, conversing about our lives and the precious memories we've created together. I am forever grateful for you.

To my sister, my yin to my yang, no words can truly express the love I have for you. We have fought side by side in the trenches of life, enduring every challenge together. To my friend, my lifelong homie, my dearest sister, thank you for your unwavering strength along the way. We may stumble, but the Garcias always rise to the challenge, resilient and united forever.

Acknowledgment

To this life, my greatest teacher, I offer my deepest gratitude for every burden, every struggle, and every tear shed along the way. These trials have forged me into a humble man, one who understands that true strength emerges from hardship. I stand before you, profoundly shaped by the lessons learned through this challenging journey. It is the majesty of the possibility of your presence that has been my guiding light in the darkest moments. For this, I am eternally grateful, knowing that it is through our struggles that we truly discover our strength and purpose.

Lord, I am but your paintbrush, shaped by your hand as you masterfully perfect each stroke. Thank you, Father, for everything you have bestowed upon me; without your tough love and guidance, I would not stand as the man I am today. You saw the warrior within me long before I ever realized it myself, igniting a fire in my spirit that propels me forward. Your unwavering presence has been my foundation, and the love I hold for you knows no bounds. I am eternally grateful for your wisdom and the strength you've instilled in me.

About the Author

The author is a remarkable individual, 40-year-old Marine veteran, athlete, mentor, and visionary. Renowned for his unwavering commitment to personal growth, he exemplifies resilience, discipline, and the courage to evolve. Having triumphed over adversity, he has rebuilt his life with purpose and clarity, driven by a heartfelt desire to inspire others to unlock their potential and seize control of their destinies.

As both a thinker and a doer, he has devoted his life to striking a balance between strength and humility, action and reflection. Through his writing, mentorship, and leadership, the author's mission is to empower others to transcend limitations and claim the fulfilling life they deserve. His voice resonates with hope, transformation, and empowerment, grounded in the belief that true victory begins within, regardless of the battles we face.

When he's not writing, the author channels his energy into boxing, fitness, and mentoring the next generation to become warriors in their own lives. With a mind as sharp as a blade and a heart full of passion, he embodies the truth that the most significant battles are those we fight and win amongst ourselves.

Contents

Before We Get Started

Welcome, dear reader. Before we embark on this journey together, I suggest that you approach these words with an open mind and an open heart. Allow yourself to receive a message that could transform the very essence of your perspective.

It all begins with our mindset. The way we see the world shapes our reality; it guides us to recognize patterns and possibilities that might otherwise remain hidden. We are creatures of habit, and within this truth lies a profound opportunity: the understanding that each of us holds the power to redefine our lives through our thoughts. This book serves as a beacon for those who seek to discover the simple yet profound truths that will unveil the true potential within.

You have everything you need to become who you wish to be in this world. All it takes is the spark of an idea and the courage to act upon it. This guide speaks to the hearts of young individuals striving to unlock their potential, encouraging them to embrace their authenticity. You are enough, just as you are. The world has no need for facades; the Lord has designed you uniquely and purposely.

Let us not squander this precious life, for it is fleeting. It's time to step into the light and savor this journey of self-discovery. By peeling back the layers, we can understand ourselves and others on a deeper level. By doing so, we gain invaluable insights that empower us to contribute meaningfully to society.

Ladies and gentlemen, I proudly present to you: "The Truth Is Not Always What It Seems."

For want of a map, the path lay shrouded in uncertainty.

For want of a path, progress crawled at a torturous pace.

For want of haste, the vital message sank into silence.

For want of the message, the warriors wavered, their resolve faltering.

For want of their strength, the battle slipped from their grasp.

And all for the want of clear direction—a source of clarity in the chaos.

The point of no Return

God is the creator of life and has gifted humanity with the power of free will. Yet the simple truth is that everything in this world is shaped by human hands, including the words we speak. In ancient Egypt, when it stood at the center of civilization, a pharaoh would proclaim, "So let it be written, so let it be done." This powerful declaration mirrors the Lord's creative utterance: "Let there be light"—and light emerged.

According to the Bible, God made us in His likeness, creating the first humans to dwell in a garden and follow His guidance. In essence, He is both their creator and their father.

If we are indeed crafted in the image of our Father, we must ask: which Father do we mean? The Lord, or our literal creators—our birth parents? This book aims to broaden your perspective, guiding you toward a deeper level of consciousness. To be true to ourselves, we must remove the blindfold of the entrenched lies that have controlled humanity's mind and begin to think beyond the manipulative force of fear.

"To truly understand something, it's essential to explore its origins."

We all know a simple word to explain and understand what happened in the distant past: History. History can be further distilled into two simple words, which can be viewed as "His-story." Here, 'His' signifies the essence of what men are given during their time on Earth, while 'story' chronicles their achievements and struggles with the gift of life. Viewed from this perspective, history is not just a timeline of events; it is a testament to the ways in which humanity has navigated creation and power.

Throughout this book, when you encounter the phrase "Side Note," take a moment to pause and reflect. These sections carry impactful messages that relate back to the heart of our journey. Each "Side Note" is carefully crafted to offer additional insight and emphasize an essential truth, guiding you to a deeper understanding and connection with the story.

To truly understand who we are, we must first explore how we arrived at this moment. How can we know our place in the world without examining our past? Let us begin to peel back the layers of the onion of existence, revealing deeper truths along the way.

Remember, once you know, you cannot go back to ignorance. Take this as food for thought as our journey into understanding begins.

"I would rather be slapped with the truth than kissed with a lie."

— Russian Proverb

A Man by Many Names

Let us begin our exploration with a figure central to human belief: Jesus Christ, known by many names:

- The Deliverer
- Messianic King
- Messiah
- Savior
- Immanuel
- The Anointed One
- Jesus of Nazareth

For over 2,000 years, He has stood as a pivotal figure in the faith known as Christianity, embodying a deep-seated yearning for connection with the divine. To understand His impact, we must first unravel the concept of the timeline. His impact is so that history is written with respect to his birth (BC) and death (AD). Let's study in detail what it means.

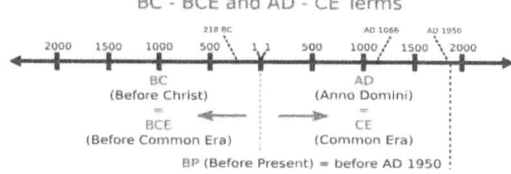

BC - BCE and AD - CE Terms

- **Anno Domini (AD):** Latin for "in the year of our Lord," this term was established to measure years from the birth of Jesus.
- **Before Christ (BC):** A designation for years before that pivotal moment.

However, in our increasingly diverse world, these terms have become less inclusive. To adopt a more neutral terminology, we now use:

- **Common Era (CE):** Replacing AD, this term reflects a broader cultural context.
- **Before Common Era (BCE):** This replaces BC, providing a secular alternative.

Why this shift, you may wonder? The reality is that approximately 68.66% of the world does not identify as Christian. Research reveals the following distribution of beliefs:

31.11% Christianity

24.90% Islam

15.58% Unaffiliated

15.16% Hinduism

6.62% Buddhism

5.61% Folk religions

0.79% Other

The terms BC and AD originate from the year 525 AD, introduced by a monk named Dionysius Exiguus, also known as Dionysius the Humble. An important point to note in examining the timeline is that there is no year zero.

Side note: Some would argue that, because of people's difficulty in understanding mathematics—particularly the concept of zero—the travelers before us simplified this by creating a calendar that transitioned from 1 BC/BCE to 1 AD/CE.

While Christians might assert that this is the year of Jesus' birth, historical analysis suggests that Jesus was born around 4 to 6 BCE. Yet, we often overlook the vast expanse of human history that preceded His arrival.

Consider notable figures such as Alexander the Great, Aristotle, Socrates, Plato, Julius Caesar, Cleopatra, and King Herod. Each is pivotal in shaping the world prior to the arrival of Jesus Christ. These leaders, thinkers, and conquerors not only influenced their immediate surroundings but also laid the groundwork for the philosophical and political frameworks that would guide human thought for centuries.

Herod, fearful of the prophecy concerning a coming Messiah during Jesus' birth, exemplifies how insecurity can drive even the most powerful to desperate actions, as seen in the Massacre of the Innocents. This tragic event serves as a grim reminder of how the perceived threat to authority can lead to moral depravity.

Each of these figures, whether through conquest, governance, or philosophical inquiry. Reflects the broader human struggle with power, legacy, and ethical dilemmas. They remind us that the pursuit of greatness often comes with profound responsibility. Their interactions with destiny and their respective societies highlight the fragility of power, the complexities of human motivation, and the enduring quest for meaning in the face of monumental change. Ultimately, they collectively shape the cultural and historical context into which Jesus would step, unveiling the majesties of his great power through belief, illustrating how each of their legacies contributed to the pattern of human history. In which I say, *"History tends to echo through time."*

The Year of the Written Word

The documentation of history allows us to understand countless events from the past, particularly since writing was perfected in the year 3300 BCE when humans marked the dawn of recorded history. You may wonder why this moment is significant. Without the ability to document events, we cannot form a coherent history. Everything preceding written records is categorized as prehistory, representing humanity's rise to the species we know today as Homo sapiens.

From the time of the dawn of writing (the first written word being around 3300 BCE) to the arrival of Jesus, estimated between 6 and 4 BCE, there existed a remarkable span of 3,294 to 3,296 years of recorded history—not including the immense expanse of prehistory.

Side Note: The importance of words cannot be overstated; they have the power to shape our beliefs, influence our actions, and even alter the course of history. Consider the case of Galileo Galilei, who endeavored to enlighten the Catholic Church about the heliocentric nature of our solar system. His scientific truths fell on deaf ears as the church clung to its narrative, which was deeply intertwined with how people understood and preserved the Word of God. This highlights how the manipulation of language can suppress the truth, guiding individuals away from enlightenment and understanding.

Language itself carries tremendous weight. Jesus spoke Aramaic and knew Hebrew, both rich languages that conveyed profound meanings. Now, think about the transition to English. Such a transition can obscure meaning and intention. For instance, the commandment "Thou shalt not murder" is infamously rendered as "Thou shalt not kill" in many translations. This subtle yet significant change not only shifts the moral implications but can profoundly impact a person's ethical compass, leading to confusion about what is right and wrong.

When words are altered or manipulated, the effects can be catastrophic. A good person striving to do right may find themselves conflicted by a statement that has been reshaped to serve a different agenda. Thus, the language we use and how it is employed by others can either liberate us or bind us to falsehoods.

We must remain vigilant about the words we choose to embrace and those we allow others to teach us. The language that instructs us can either promote freedom and understanding or lead us into the incarceration of the mind. Choose wisely, for the power of words is profound, and their impact can last a lifetime.

If you truly wish to delve into the depths of existence, consider this: our planet dates back approximately 4.5 billion years (4,500 million). As you grapple with this extraordinarily vast timeframe, let's discuss how we categorize human civilization into distinct eras.

The eras are:

Stone Age (Prehistory)

Bronze Age

Iron Age

Classical Antiquity: The era of Jesus on Earth

The Stone Age was the beginning of the human experiment. Reaching beyond 2.5 million years ago until the year 3300 BCE. During this time, humans begin to develop societies, creating tools and the utilization of stones to create weapons to hunt for food. In this time, people are a primitive bunch, finding ways to survive with basic essentials. This era is a keyhole into the lives of our ancestors as they found ways to adapt to the ever-changing environments.

Side note: I wish to illustrate our progression over time by presenting a structured overview of the key moments that capture the footprints of humanity throughout history.

Australopithecus: One of the earliest known hominins, it lived around 4 million to 2 million years ago and is significant for showing bipedalism. Bipedalism is a foundational aspect of human evolution that has had profound implications for our species' development, behavior, and way of life.

Homo habilis: Known as "handyman," this species emerged about 2.4 million years ago and is believed to be the first maker of stone tools.

Homo erectus: Living from about 1.9 million years ago to as recently as 110,000 years ago, this species displayed more advanced tools and was the first to use fire and possibly engage in early forms of social organization.

Neanderthals (Homo neanderthalensis): Existing approximately 400,000 to 40,000 years ago, Neanderthals were closely related to modern humans and exhibited complex behaviors, including burial rituals and tool-making.

Homo sapiens: Biologically modern humans, appearing around 300,000 years ago, known for advanced cognitive abilities, language, and the ability to create art and engage in complex social structures.

The Agricultural Revolution: Also known as the Neolithic Revolution, this period (around 10,000 BCE) marks a significant transformation where humans shifted from nomadic lifestyles to settled farming communities, changing social structures and leading to the rise of civilizations.

The Industrial Revolution: Initiating in the late 18th century and into the 19th century, this transformation encompassed technological advancements that drastically altered human society, economy, and culture through industrialization.

The Bronze Age followed the Stone Age, beginning approximately around 3300 BCE and lasting until about 1200 BCE. This period is defined by the introduction of metalworking techniques, specifically the alloy of copper and tin known as bronze. Societies began to develop more complex structures, including early forms of government, trade routes, and written language, fundamentally transforming human civilization.

Side note: the collapse of the Bronze Age was due to many factors, from Invasion and migration, natural disasters, and economic decline, with the centralized power no longer in control of the people. Major civilizations like Greece, Egypt, and Anatolia disappeared almost instantaneously, and what followed was the introduction of the Greek Dark Ages, AKA the Iron Age.

The Iron Age represented a period of enlightenment as humanity sought to emerge from darkness and embrace the growth of civilization. In this time period, the world's most famous legendary tales supposedly took place.

- The Jewish Torah
  - Moses (400 BCE)
- The Greek Iliad (written by a poet of the time, Homer, 1184 BCE)
  - Achilles
  - Agamemnon
  - Hector
  - Patroclus

Side note: 1184 – 400 = 784 years until the mention of Moses; let how much time went by sink in. We say a lot happens in a year; what about 784 years, and this is just the Iron age.

Notable countries of the time.

Carthage * Rome * Sparta * Judah * Athens

Side note: The Greek Dark Ages lasted for 400 years, a time known for its violence and the disruption of cultural practices.

Now we delve into the heart of human history: The Classical Antiquity era. Spanning from approximately 500 BCE to the fall of the Western Roman Empire in 476 CE, this period stands out as a remarkable chapter in the story of civilization. It is characterized by the emergence of influential cultures, particularly those of the Greeks and Romans, and is often regarded as a pinnacle of cultural achievement. This era also coincides with the life of Jesus Christ, whose teachings and influence profoundly shaped religious thought and laid the groundwork for Western civilization, facilitating a transition into subsequent historical epochs.

I hold a particular fondness for this time period, as its significance in forming the foundations of Western civilization cannot be overstated. Allow me to introduce you to some extraordinary leaders and pivotal events that not only shaped the course of history but also inspired humanity to move forward through time.

Main Leaders of this Era:

Alexander the Great

Ramses II

Attila the Hun

Constantine

Marcus Aurelius

Julius Caesar

Socrates

Plato

Jesus of Nazareth

Cleopatra

Diogenes of Sinope

Emperor Wu of the Han

Hannibal Barca

Octavian (Augustus)

Pericles

Cicero

Major Events

Assassination of Julius Caesar

The Peloponnesian War

Discovery of the Rosetta Stone

The Founding of Constantinople

Fall of Rome

The Council of Nicaea

Birth and Death of Jesus

The spread of Hellenistic culture

Bubonic Plague in Athens

The construction of the Great Wall of China

Golden Age of Athens

Introduction of Coin Currency

Development of the Silk Road

The extraordinary efforts of these leaders and the significance of these events reveal the intricate richness of Classical Antiquity, an era characterized by deep thought, innovation, and cultural vibrancy, which continues to shape our world today.

A noteworthy figure of Classical Antiquity was Marcus Aurelius, my favorite ruler of Rome. Renowned as the last of the Five Good Emperors, he authored Meditations, a journal that has since been published and continues to guide seekers of wisdom today. His understanding of Stoicism deeply influenced my perspective on human behavior, emphasizing that we have control over our actions by embracing the Stoic virtues of Courage, Temperance, Justice, and Wisdom—principles that enable us to live purposefully and with integrity.

"Accept the things to which fate binds you, and love the people with whom fate brings you together, but do so with all your heart."

— Marcus Aurelius

The Influence of a Father

Let's turn our focus back to Jesus. This segment invites open-mindedness and a bit of logical exploration. Everything that we know about Jesus is also in written form. We know that Jesus is referred to as the Son of God, born to a young woman named Mary, who, by most accounts, was between 14 and 16 years old at the time of His birth, with some sources suggesting she may have been as young as 13.

Considering the concept of the Almighty and His infinite power, one wonders about the nature of His embodiment in such a young lady. The notion that she could conceive without traditional means—without a male partner—can seem unrealistic. A more probable scenario might suggest that a prominent spiritual leader of the time was involved in an arrangement to foster a child who would ultimately lead the early church into what became Christianity.

This perspective considers how people viewed innocence and spirituality during that era; a perceptive individual could easily manipulate the prevailing beliefs and fears of the populace. Indeed, the passage of time must have felt urgent, as many likely sensed a countdown with no clear understanding of what lay beyond—this fear of the unknown can be profoundly unsettling.

If you recall the end of 1999, you might share my sense of trepidation as the Y2K phenomenon approached. A chilling fear surrounded the idea that as the clock struck midnight on December 31, 1999, we might revert to the Stone Age. Y2K was anticipated to wreak havoc on computer systems, potentially dismantling banking infrastructures and power plants. The anticipation of unresolved system failures created a collective anxiety that was both palpable and nerve-wracking.

Think about it.

In today's time, we see how a father might train his son to become a footballer, a boxer, or excel in any field that requires dedication and time to master. Typically, the father would begin this training early, instilling his preferences—teaching him which teams to support, explaining the nuances of the game, and sharing his own philosophy on the play. He might show clips of past players he admired, encouraging his son to emulate their techniques. After all, we know that the earlier you begin honing a skill, the faster you excel.

The early stages of a child's development are pivotal, representing a foundational period where programming begins. During this time, parents and guardians play a vital role in imprinting their values and beliefs onto the child's developing mind. Children instinctively seek guidance from those around them, relying on caregivers to teach them how to navigate the world. This natural phenomenon, known as social learning, underscores our inherent desire to absorb the behaviors and attitudes of others. By learning from their environment and the people within it, children hope to acquire knowledge and skills that will aid them in understanding and managing the complexities of life.

As members of society, it is essential to engage with history from a variety of perspectives. Doing so enriches our understanding of one another and fosters empathy, allowing us to connect on a deeper level. Education should not be viewed solely as a tool for personal growth; rather, it plays a crucial role in shaping us into informed and engaged citizens.

Our inclination to see the world only through our own lens is one of the greatest challenges we face. It limits our ability to understand the diverse experiences and perspectives of others. By confronting this limitation, we open ourselves up to a broader comprehension of humanity and the elaborate design of history that has shaped our present.

Engaging with different viewpoints not only broadens our worldview but also equips us with the tools necessary for meaningful dialogue and collaboration within our communities. Every interaction, every lesson learned from history, has the potential to inspire deeper understanding and guide us toward positive social change.

Everyday learning is vital. It empowers us to challenge preconceived notions and confront biases, paving the way for a more inclusive society by committing to lifelong learning, whether through formal education, personal study, or intercultural experiences. We cultivate the curiosity and resilience needed to navigate an increasingly complex world. Let us strive to value education not just for ourselves but for the collective good as we become better equipped to contribute thoughtfully to our diverse communities.

We have a unique opportunity to leverage our understanding of history to foster growth and connection in our communities. Through the study of history, we develop empathy and enhance our ability to think critically about the lives of those around us. This understanding is invaluable, benefiting not only ourselves but also the broader fabric of society.

We must confront complex ideas such as civilization through a lens grounded in emotional intelligence and maturity. By exploring the history of money and economics, we can better understand the motivations behind economic systems and the impacts of wealth distribution on societal inequalities. In the same way, examining the core concepts of science and biology is frequently viewed as the language of the divine. It provides us with insights into the natural world and our place within it, emphasizing the interdependence of all living things.

Understanding how environmental changes impact societal stability is paramount. As we have spoken about past civilizations, most, if not all, were due to the decline of environmental factors. We obtain lessons that are crucial in addressing contemporary issues such as climate change and resource management. This knowledge encourages us to advocate for sustainable practices and to collaborate on solutions that promote both ecological health and community resilience.

Side note: We must first look back and comprehend past events in order to make informed decisions about the present and future. The future truly lies in your hands!

As you embark on this journey, my wish is that with maturity, you will possess the bravery to rethink or surpass the beliefs handed down to you, fostering your own perspectives and ideas.

Many individuals falter, adhering to conformist ideals, ultimately failing to reach their true potential. Some reference the "10,000-Hour Rule," which suggests that mastery of any skill is achieved after approximately 10,000 hours of dedicated practice. While I do not assert that mastering any skill strictly requires this amount of time, the essence remains clear: practice makes perfect.

Putting the 'practice makes perfect' into action, imagine yourself as a child born in Bethlehem, constantly told that you are Jesus, the Son of God, the Messiah, the future leader of the Jewish people and the Church. You are the deliverer destined to lift the burden of mankind's sins, and one day, you will be called to sacrifice yourself to ensure the survival of an idea—Christianity—through the ages.

Side note: A nod to Rome, the center of the universe during that time (6/4 BCE to April 30, 33 CE), a subject we'll explore later.

When you are raised with the belief that you are destined for greatness, you are inclined to adopt that identity, trusting those who affirm it. This is a clear example of early programming.

Many claim to know what Jesus's childhood was like. Consider the challenge of being moved from place to place by your parents, fleeing a mad king—King Herod—who sought your life. I believe Jesus was accumulating his "10,000 hours" from birth, embodying a unique promise amidst the immense expectations placed upon him. Even as a child, he must have exhibited remarkable wisdom and sophistication. He lived his early life with grace and eloquence, embodying the principle that faith is more potent than mere words. Through his actions, he demonstrated that ideas can transcend time.

The Elephant in the Room

During my time in the Marines, I participated in a mission called Cobra Gold, where we traveled to Thailand to train alongside the Thai Marines. This experience allowed us to exchange knowledge and skills. We taught them tactical maneuvers, like how to dismount from trucks and establish perimeters, while they educated us on jungle warfare—a truly enriching experience.

Side note: One of the most memorable moments came at the conclusion of the training. The Thai Marines showcased their bravery by capturing a live cobra and dropping it in front of us. I was terrified but managed to conceal my fear. One particular Thai Marine, demonstrating agility akin to that of a professional boxer, seized the cobra by the throat and swiftly severed its head before my eyes. The instructor I was with called me over, and this Thai Marine—who I had grown fond of—invited me to kneel. As he held the severed head, he dripped the warm blood of the cobra into my mouth, declaring, "You and the cobra are one; now we are family." This gesture struck a profound chord with me. –

"When in Rome, do as the Romans do."

— English proverb.

There, I discovered the profound spirituality of the place, especially through the lessons taught by the local customs. One particularly striking lesson was about elephants, sacred animals in Thai culture. From birth, these powerful creatures are tethered with a simple 6-foot rope. This same rope serves them throughout their lives.

What's remarkable is that these elephants learn early on that they cannot break free. As babies, they lack the strength to pull away and become psychologically conditioned to believe that the rope is stronger than they are. This conditioning holds their incredible power in check, and as adults, they submit to the limitations imposed by that rope, never attempting to escape despite their immense physical strength.

Side note: This serves as a poignant reminder of what can happen when one has a poor teacher; they may never recognize their true potential. It is only when we take that first step in faith that we begin to uncover the wonders of life. If that elephant, upon reaching adulthood, had the courage to venture beyond that sixth step, it would discover its strength to break free from the stake that binds it. The hardest step is often that leap into the unknown—the point where fear resides. However, freedom is just beyond that threshold. **Never give up! Never surrender!**

Now, if we can impose such limitations on an elephant, imagine the potential we could realize in children. Think of Jesus (the elephant), shaped by a lifetime of being told that he was meant to represent a cause—to inspire humanity to a new understanding. He was tasked with carrying the weight of mankind's sins and ultimately sacrificing himself as an example of unwavering faith.

Consider the magnitude of faith required to endure the knowledge that, in the end, everyone would abandon him. Yet, he still mustered the strength to fulfill his mission. His journey illustrates the importance of seeing something through to the end. If he had faltered in his faith and not carried out his purpose, it's unlikely we would be reflecting on his bravery over 2000 years later. His sacrifice for the sake of mankind ensured our spiritual freedom and awareness of the vital importance of change.

Side note: In summary, Jesus's brief life and brutal death were pivotal in conveying that the only path to salvation was through him. His message of hope and the prospect of everlasting life spread from Judea across the Roman Empire and ultimately, around the world. And keep in mind this was only in the early CE (33). –

A Brief History Lesson on Christianity

Christianity developed in Judea (present-day Israel) during the 1st Century. The Bible, which encompasses both the Old and New Testaments, reached its final form with the completion of the New Testament around 95 CE. It took 12 years after Jesus's death to finalize the New Testament, followed by an additional 50 years to finalize its compilation.

The Old Testament, also known as the Jewish Bible or Hebrew Bible, consists of collections of ancient religious writings by the Israelites. The New Testament serves as an addition to the Old Testament, originally penned in Greek. It documents the life and teachings of Jesus, interpreted through the perspectives of the authors Matthew, Mark, Luke, and John.

Notably, the creation of the New Testament was primarily the work of Jewish Christians or Jewish disciples of Christ living in Rome. Christianity traces its origins to the ministry of Jesus, born around 6 or 4 BCE. He was a Jewish teacher—often referred to as a rabbi—a healer who proclaimed the imminent Kingdom of God. Jesus was crucified in Jerusalem between the years 30 and 33 CE under the governance of the Roman province of Judea.

Side note: The location of Jesus' death is Golgotha, which means "place of the skull."

Pontius Pilate, the Roman governor at that time, found himself in a dilemma influenced by the religious leaders who despised Jesus for threatening the fragile peace imposed by Roman authority. While Pilate recognized Jesus's significance, he was torn by the pressure to eliminate what many saw as a threat. Ultimately, he left the decision to the people, offering them a choice between Jesus and a known criminal, Barabbas. The crowd, swayed by the religious leaders, chose the criminal over Jesus.

Side note: This part of the story evokes a quote from Nucky Thompson in Boardwalk Empire: "First rule of politics, Kiddo… Never let the truth get in the way of a good story." What's the lesson here? "Believe half of what you see and none of what you hear." –

Jesus was subsequently arrested, and from that moment until his crucifixion, he endured one of the most humiliating, gruesome, and disturbing forms of torture imaginable. Ultimately, he was nailed to a cross and stabbed with a weapon known as the Spear of Destiny, bleeding out for all to witness.

After his death, Jesus was regarded by Christians as a martyr, and the very fear Pilate sought to avoid manifested. Enraged by Pilate's decision to crucify Jesus, Rome ordered him and his soldiers home to live out their days in disgrace. By executing Jesus, they had unwittingly destabilized the region, contributing to the emergence of a new religion—Christianity—that would spread throughout the empire and influence beliefs for centuries to come.

Initially, Christianity was small and unorganized, promising personal salvation after death, which was attainable only through belief in Jesus as the Son of God. Decades after Jesus's death, the Apostle Paul wrote numerous letters that became part of the New Testament. A Roman citizen himself, Paul endeavored to articulate what it meant to be Christian, fostering understanding within small communities.

It wasn't until 313 CE that Roman Emperor Constantine granted Christianity legal status through the Edict of Milan, signaling a significant shift away from the pantheon of Roman gods and goddesses (Paganism) represented by figures like Jupiter, Juno, and Minerva. ("Jupiter embodies power, Juno symbolizes love, and Minerva represents wisdom; together they inspire us to reach for greatness in all aspects of life.") A few decades later, in 380 CE, Emperor Theodosius I established the Nicene Creed as the orthodox doctrine for Christianity, officially making it the religion of the Roman Empire through the Edict of Thessalonica.

Side note: In my opinion, this marked the beginning of the decline of the great Roman Empire.

Christianity:

- Faith: Belief in God and spiritual conviction.
- Grace: Unmerited favor from God, symbolizing compassion and forgiveness.
- Salvation: Deliverance from sin and its consequences.
- Redemption: The act of being saved from sin, error, or evil.
- Hope: Anticipation of a positive future grounded in faith.
- Love: Central to teachings, emphasizing selflessness and compassion.
- Community: Focus on gathering and supporting each other in faith.

Paganism:

- Nature: Reverence for the natural world and its cycles.
- Ritual: Ceremonies to honor deities and mark seasonal changes.
- Deity: Belief in multiple gods/goddesses, each with specific powers.
- Balance: The importance of harmony between nature, self, and the cosmos.

- Fertility: Often central to practices, emphasizing abundance and growth.
- Tradition: Strong ties to heritage and ancestral worship.
- Freedom: Personal choice in spiritual practices and beliefs.

To conclude the history of Christianity, it is essential to recognize that it emerged from Jewish traditions and was significantly shaped by Roman cultural and political structures. Christianity was profoundly influenced by Rome; without its support and infrastructure, Christianity might never have existed, and the story of Jesus could have faded into obscurity long ago.

To Know Thyself

Throughout history, those in power have proclaimed themselves the chosen ones, but everyone who has ever existed is, in fact, a chosen one. A great battle raged long before we took our first breath. The moment we open our eyes to the world is a gift—a reward for winning that fight. You triumphed over millions of potential competitors for the right to exist. Recognizing this simple yet profound truth can bring a sense of peace, as your first major battle has already been won. If only we could appreciate the glory of that initial act.

It's a waste to strive to be something you're not when the Lord has crafted you beautifully, just as you are. If you cannot recognize your own worth, why did you struggle so hard to enter this world, only to forget its simplicity? You might as well have given someone else the chance at life, wasting your precious time on Earth.

We are akin to a drop of water, first pushed from a spout, falling until we merge with the sea of time. Once we blend with the beyond, our earthly experience ends. It is in understanding how we utilize our time during that fall that we will be remembered. Would we aspire to live like Jesus, who dedicated his life to instructing, helping, and inspiring others to become the best versions of themselves? He stood firm in his beliefs and performed miraculous feats. Ultimately, the choice is yours: who you wish to be and what you want to accomplish is determined by your thoughts and perspectives.

Life, along with the beauty of death, enriches existence. The idea of eternity loses its allure if we cannot appreciate the sweetness of completing a life with death. Knowing that I will die one day brings me peace; I embrace the inevitability. Having faced death on several occasions, it seems the Universe had other plans for me. Perhaps my journey through pain, heartbreak, loss, suffering, and loneliness has prepared me to share these words, reaching those who ask, "Why me?" or "How could you, Lord?"

We often point fingers, shifting blame away from ourselves. In truth, the one we must hold accountable is the person in the mirror. Because the greatest trick the devil ever pulled was convincing the world that he didn't exist. Yet, the true devil is often the person gazing back at us in the mirror. Many struggle to accept hard truths but to evolve, we must conform to the simplest truths. We are who we are in this world, so let us strive to make the best of it.

What is the simplest truth of the world? It is the concept of Heaven and Hell, often shaped by our own subconscious beliefs about what we deserve. We assume that God orchestrates our actions and that we lack control over our futures as if everything is predetermined. But what if God desires us to judge ourselves and realize that we hold the reins to our destiny? What if our experiences arise from our own actions rather than some cosmic plan?

Let me ask you a question: what does it mean to be part of something? To care, to wake up with purpose, and to envision possibilities yet to be explored? As a young man coming from nothing, I thought I knew a lot, but looking back, I see now how little I truly understood. When you don't read or ponder the world around you, you risk failing to ask the right questions, as human emotions cloud your decision-making.

My father was present, but not in the way I needed him to be. He was a hard man, lacking patience and entangled in a life far from the norm. Although he fulfilled his responsibilities—providing food, clothing, and shelter—he neglected to teach me what it means to be a man of value. Instead, he taught me to prioritize gain, to seize what I wanted without remorse.

Though those lessons hold great value now in a world rife with corruption, as a young man, I pretended to be someone I wasn't to impress my father. In his eyes, I was a weak link, unlike him. I was more like my mother—full of love, joy, and care—yet robbed of my innocence while growing up in Miami. "There are no such things as friends," my dad would say. Now, I understand why he felt that way, given the life he led. Yet, as a young man and even today, I've struggled to form meaningful relationships, burdened by the wisdom I acquired too early.

Looking back, it wasn't until I began to read that I started seeing things from a different perspective. My initial thought, as I ventured down the rabbit hole, was: how does this all work? I turned to God, as I had many times before, asking Him about the purpose of my life.

At first, there was silence—days spent in seclusion, deep in empty thought. But like a wave rising, my questions led to curiosity, and curiosity sparked immense research. I began by exploring the human body, seeking to understand the complexities behind even the simplest gestures, like moving my hand. In the end, I found this organism to be utterly fascinating, for as the mind thinks, the body acts.

Yet, I felt like a spring coiled tight, full of potential but stuck in that position. I was left dreaming but never doing, losing the precious gift of life to Father Time. The regrets flooded in: I wish I had done this; I wish I had tried that. To live a life filled with such wishes feels like the greatest sin of all.

"It is a shame for a man to grow old without seeing the beauty
and strength of which his body is capable."

— Socrates

Fear often hinders us from achieving greatness. As one of my mentors wisely stated,

"We suffer more in the mind than we do in reality."

— Seneca

So, back to the question: what does it mean to be a part of something? The first thought that should arise is, how can I ever truly be part of anything if I don't even know myself? It's only when we understand ourselves that we can genuinely contribute to anything.

"To know thyself is the beginning of wisdom."

— Socrates

The Fruit from the Tree

Every great book must have a story that hooks the audience, inviting them on an exciting journey. In the Bible, that story begins in the book of Genesis with the Garden of Eden. Before we proceed, let's break down the Lord's attributes:

- Omnipotent: Unlimited Power and Potential
- Omnibenevolent: Perfect or Unlimited Goodness
- Omniscience: The state of Knowing Everything

He is the Alpha and the Omega—the beginning and the end, the One who is, who always was, and who is still to come, the Almighty One.

God created Adam and tasked him with living freely in the Garden of Eden, naming all the animals that resided there. Adam had the freedom to roam and enjoy his life with a single command: he must not eat from the tree of the knowledge of good and evil. The Lord sought to create a companion for Adam, causing him to fall into a deep sleep, from which He took a rib to fashion a woman named Eve. Upon seeing her, Adam declared, "This is now bone of my bone and flesh of my flesh; she shall be called woman because she was taken out of man."

Now, imagine a man and a woman living in pure bliss, walking around without shame, experiencing life that is free from pain and full of blessings.

Eve, possessing the same knowledge as Adam, understood she could do as she pleased except eat from the forbidden tree. One day, while Adam cared for the animals, Eve found herself drawn to the forbidden tree. **Side note:** Many don't realize that in the Garden of Eden, there were two trees:

- The Tree of Life
- The Tree of Knowledge of Good and Evil –

Curiosity led Eve to think about the very action she was advised to avoid. At this pivotal moment, a serpent—believed to be Lucifer, the Prince of Darkness—tempted her. She embraced the suggestion, letting it consume her thoughts. This marks the first act of temptation and the beginning of the end of paradise, as Eve is seduced by a third party. **Side note:** There is a crucial message at this moment that all men should understand, but I will delve into that **Later.**

Eve ate the fruit and fell for the first lie ever told by the serpent, who claimed that if she consumed it, she "would become as God, knowing good from evil." After eating, she felt different, and out of fear of what she had done, she persuaded Adam to eat, too. Despite knowing it was wrong, Adam consumed the fruit without realizing Eve had been deceived by the serpent.

This dilemma underscores the phrase "ignorance is bliss." By eating the fruit, they gained the knowledge they were not meant to have. Over time, this newfound awareness led to feelings of shame, and they tried to cover their nakedness. Consequently, they experienced a spiritual death due to their disobedience. When the Lord returned to the garden, He could not sense His children. When He called out, they appeared covered in palm leaves or other leafy items, and He understood at that moment what they had done. As a result of their disobedience, they were banished from the garden and forced to contend with the knowledge of good and evil.

While I don't interpret this story literally, I believe it serves as a guide to understanding human behavior and the consequences of straying from Jesus's teachings. Misguided agendas can lead to innocent lives being lost in vain.

Side note: A pertinent example is the story of the Children's Crusade (1212), in which some claim thousands of children participated—akin to the size of ten Marine Corps battalions. Organized by a 12-year-old shepherd boy named Stephen, persuaded by a priest who claimed Heaven appointed him to recover the Holy Sepulcher in Jerusalem, these children set forth without weapons, carrying banners and crosses. They believed they could convert Muslims through persuasion and divine intervention.

However, leaders like Saladin, a prominent Muslim figure, were also dedicated to reclaiming Jerusalem. The idea that children could simply walk into the Holy City and request its handover was naive, and sadly, hundreds of thousands of children were led to their deaths due to the manipulation of religious figures pushing them toward historical folly.

The journey began in France and passed through the French and Swiss Alps, where many died from hunger and freezing temperatures. Those who reached Genoa faced a language barrier and were cruelly tricked by pirates, ending up sold into slavery or worse. This occurrence highlights how unrealistic plans can lead to catastrophe.

The essential takeaway is that Jesus spoke in parables, often weaving stories within stories. At the end of these narratives, we must ask ourselves: did we grasp the message?

I encourage you to broaden your perspective and go beyond your programming. One of the Lord's attributes is omniscience—the state of knowing everything. He knew that Adam and Eve would disobey Him yet still placed the temptation of that tree before them. This indicates that He knew all the events leading to today.

As you think about this simple truth, understand that temptation exists regardless of whether you choose to acknowledge it or not. In the end, it is up to you to decide whether to follow Adam and Eve or to become a person strong enough to resist outside influences. Strength comes from making choices, not simply reacting to what's happening around you. Overcoming your temptations requires self-awareness and the will to stay true to your values.

"**Later**" — Let's revisit the actions of Eve and the message behind her seduction. Men, we must recognize a fundamental truth about women: they are emotional beings. While this emotional depth can give women an advantage over men, it can also lead to irrational decisions, making them vulnerable to the persuasive words of others.

One important aspect of the Bible is that it was primarily written with men in mind. It often neglects the complexities of women's roles beyond that of service, as derived from the narrative of Eve being created from Adam's rib. And if we are to be honest with ourselves, women have endured a prolonged reign of subjugation that mirrors the harsh realities of slavery. This uncompromising reality has profoundly shaped historical interpretations, further limiting recognition of women's contributions and influence.

Perspective is Important

In today's world, many people crave instant gratification. Most people fall victim to this idea, never realizing their potential because they fail to understand that meaningful things take time to grow. Take love, for example, which is often confused with lust. Love is not something that happens overnight; it involves endurance, sacrifice, and a commitment that requires all of you. Embracing what you love, even when faced with challenges, helps you appreciate its true power. When used correctly, love can inspire extraordinary actions because it acts as an everlasting source of energy.

Side note: Be cautious with love, as it can lead to foolish decisions. Lust has a way of blinding us to the realities before our eyes, causing us to waste time and pieces of ourselves. So, be mindful of whom you declare your love for because love can both uplift and hurt.

Perspective is a skill you develop over time through experience. You don't know what you're capable of until you try. For example, when talking to someone of the opposite sex for the first time, you may feel anxious, with sweaty palms and a loss for words. However, with practice, rejection becomes something you learn to overcome. Remember, when one door closes, countless others remain to be opened. A "no" is just the beginning, and learning how to express it properly can lead to a "yes." Anything worth having is often difficult to attain. Accept the challenge and strive to understand the purpose of life, which fundamentally revolves around self-discovery. Once you know who you are, the world around you will too; your presence will command respect without you having to say a word.

I once watched my son playing video games for hours and realized he was spending too much time on that machine. I told him, "Son, if your video game character has a better life than you do, that's a problem. If you channeled as much energy into your homework as you do in playing that game, you'd likely be a straight-A student."

During my pursuit of a master's degree, I learned an important lesson: "Education in the absence of the means through which technology will be involved is hard on the student." This means that physiological and mental abilities can be developed when new subjects are presented effectively. Relying only on technology as a savior is akin to explaining how a computer works over the phone to someone who has never seen one. The real benefit comes from hands-on experience—the "tools"—which help the learner develop new skills.

In my son's case, the "means/mass" was the game controller. He could see, feel, and hear it, all of which are critical components of the dopamine rush experienced even before he started playing. Once the TV turned on and the sounds of the game filled the room, instant gratification was achieved, causing everything else to fall by the wayside.

As a father, it bothered me that instead of fulfilling his responsibilities, which likely felt like chores, he turned to that controller for his "fix." Watching him lose time in front of the screen made me reflect on how many of us do the same. We waste time in various ways. We escape in different forms through drug addiction, alcoholism, binge-watching shows, social media, and partying every weekend, all to avoid life's responsibilities. Later, we find ourselves asking, "Why me, Lord? How could you let this happen?"

Remember, where you are now is the result of the decisions you made five years ago, and the accumulation of missed opportunities is the price of your suffering.

Opportunity Cost and Growth

Let's take a moment to think about this. Opportunity cost is one of the most crucial concepts to understand if you wish to be successful in life. We must accept that everything worth pursuing comes with a cost, and that cost is far more valuable than gold, silver, money, or even relationships; it is time. Time is our most precious commodity, the one resource that, once spent, cannot be recovered. Recognizing its value encourages us to invest it wisely in pursuits that truly matter. Opportunities are fleeting windows; you either invest your time to prepare for them or risk missing out. In the end, your life is defined by those key moments. The way you spend your time will determine the opportunities you have tomorrow.

As I pondered how to reach my son on a deeper level, I struggled to devise a mass strong enough to overshadow the thrill of having that controller in his hands. Then, an idea struck me: think like a tree. As this concept blossomed in my mind, I began to connect every aspect of a tree to our lesson. A revelation hit me—I would use a seed as my mass.

I asked my son to put down the controller and accompany me to Home Depot. Before we reached the garden section, I made sure he could connect the dots by engaging all of his senses. I wanted him to hear, feel, smell, and touch, just as he did with his video game controller.

As we entered the garden section, he asked, "Dad, what are we doing here?" I replied, "I want a tree." He responded, "Okay, what type of tree do you want?" I answered, "I want a big one, and I want it now. Please choose a bag of seeds so I can get my tree."

Several things were happening at that moment: he was mentally and physically involved in the work he was doing. He picked out a bag of seeds, and I had him pay at the counter to help him understand the concept of possession. It means more when you navigate through the obstacles to accomplish a task.

Once we returned home, he naturally asked to resume playing his game. I reminded him politely, "We aren't finished with getting my tree." So, we headed to the backyard, where I had him dig a hole using his hands and a small garden shovel to bury the seed.

After that, he asked, "Okay, Dad, what now?" I replied, "I want my tree now!" Confusion filled his eyes as he looked at the spot where he had buried the seed and then back at me. "Dad, you're mistaken; I don't think that's how it works," he replied. "What do you mean?" I pressed. "You planted the seed; I want my tree now!" He chuckled and said, "No, Dad, it takes time for that to happen." I laughed and agreed, "Exactly! Instant gratification might provide short-term pleasure, much like playing your video game, but it won't save you from the consequences of ignoring your responsibilities."

"I wanted my tree right now, son, but anything worth having requires time, love, patience, and attentiveness. In this life, we must tackle the things we don't enjoy so we can find peace while doing what we love."

At the end of this lesson, I offered my son a perspective enriched with insight, foresight, oversight, and hindsight. I emphasized that insight allows us to understand our experiences deeply, foresight helps us anticipate future challenges and opportunities, oversight ensures we stay vigilant and accountable in our actions, and hindsight offers valuable lessons learned from our past decisions. Together, these elements create a framework for making thoughtful choices in life, encouraging him to embrace each moment as a chance for growth and understanding. I assigned him the task of caring for the seed, allowing him to truly appreciate the significance of the experience.

The act of planting the seed engaged all of his senses, making the moment much more powerful. The seed he placed in the ground was also a seed planted in his mind. As a caring father, I understand that the more

I care for, love, nurture, advise, and instruct him, the more that mental seed will flourish.

The lesson of the tree is clear: nothing worth having is achieved overnight. It takes time to nurture something of importance as it grows. Therefore, I urged him to stop wasting time on insignificant matters, for life is fleeting—nothing more than a blink of an eye. If you allow yourself to become distracted, you might miss out on what truly matters. Focusing on what truly matters helps you grow and achieve your goals, just like a tree grows with care. Time is a resource that, once lost, cannot be regained. So, it is important to use it wisely.

"Death is nothing, but to live defeated and inglorious is to die daily. If a man has not discovered something that he will die for, he isn't fit to live."

— Napoleon Bonaparte

"When your time comes to die, be not like those whose hearts
are filled with fear of death, so that when their time comes, they
weep and pray for a little more time to live their lives over again
in a different way. Sing your death song and die like a hero going
home."

— Tecumseh

Use Your Time Wisely!

In this journey, which we've undertaken together, we've explored the depths of existence, the value of time, and the delicate balance between temptation and responsibility. As we explore our lives, we are constantly faced with choices that define who we are and who we aspire to be.

Remember that every moment is an opportunity, a chance to grow, to love, and to contribute meaningfully to the world around us. Whether you choose hesitation or step boldly into the light of your potential, the power to shape your destiny lies within you.

As we reflect on the wisdom of those who came before us—be it Socrates, Tecumseh, or even the lessons of Adam and Eve—we must ask ourselves: what will we do with the time we have? Will we live in fear and keep waiting for an uncertain end? Or will we take on life, sing our own death song, and go home as the heroes of our own stories?

The choice is yours. Make it count.

Fortis Fortuna Adiuvat

As we come to a close, let's remember the saying, "Fortis Fortuna Adiuvat," or "Fortune favors the bold." Life rewards those who are willing to take risks, step outside their comfort zones, and pursue their passions with courage and conviction. Facing challenges helps you grow and find new chances, and taking bold steps can turn your dream into reality.

In a world filled with uncertainties, remember that it is the brave who carve their own paths and create their own destinies. Will you be one of them?

As you reflect on your journey, seize each day as an opportunity to act with intention and purpose. Accept the challenges, learn from failures, and no matter how small they are, celebrate your victories. Your story is waiting to be written, and the world is eagerly waiting for your contribution.

So, step boldly into your future, and let your life be a testament to the strength and beauty of living with purpose.

A Story from the Old Man

Self-actualization is the idea of shaping and mastering time and space, bending them to your will to expand the essence of your being. At this level of brain activity, you become an advanced being, possessing complete control over your mind, body, and spirit.

Before my grandfather passed away, he shared a magnificent story about the divine and its intentions for humanity. He explained that a human being is composed of three interconnected entities: the mind, the body, and the soul. The soul serves as our connection to divinity, allowing us to absorb inspiration that helps us navigate the journey of life. The body, much like the mind, operates according to its own desires; it performs tasks and seeks relevance in existence. Understanding this relevance and utilizing it to your advantage is crucial.

We are avatars given a remarkable organism to think and move. It's important to recognize what these aspects mean: the mind functions like a computer, processing information as binary code—zeros and ones. While the mind seeks knowledge, the body yearns to experience life, often leading to choices that provide temporary pleasure but may have detrimental consequences if not managed properly.

When both the body and mind understand their roles, you can take control and move in a unified direction rather than being pulled into conflicting ways of thinking and being. Once this path is clear, the body moves in harmony with the mind, which serves as an endless source of computation and insight. If only we could grasp the true majesty of this organism that the Lord has provided us to utilize while we inhabit this plane—when the three entities exist in unity, they work in unison, empowering us to harness our abilities at will.

Enrique A. Garcia

July 15, 1934

October 12, 2011

www.ingramcontent.com/pod-product-compliance
Lightning Source LLC
Chambersburg PA
CBHW051239120626
46547CB00014B/1720